TIME-OUT
for Children

Barbara Albers Hill

Avery Publishing Group
Garden City Park, New York

Cover Design: William Gonzalez and Rudy Shur
In-house Editor: Jennifer Santo

ISBN 0-89529-772-8

Printed in the United States of America

10   9   8   7   6   5   4   3   2   1

Contents

Preface

Four-year-old Laura is fascinated by her mother's cosmetics. The child isn't allowed to handle the makeup without supervision, but she cannot seem to stay away from the dressing table. Every few days, Laura gives in to temptation and adorns herself with smears of color. Laura's mother scolds and punishes her daughter on each occasion, but extra baths, cancelled play dates, and missed desserts have had little effect. Today, Laura showed up for lunch with stripes of eye shadow all over her face.

Three things are happening in Laura's

house that practically guarantee continued raids on her mother's makeup. First, the child is tempted beyond her limits of self-control by the sights and smells of the cosmetics on the dressing table. Second, she earns at least ten minutes of her mother's uninterrupted time—and an earnest talking-to from her father—with each foray into the forbidden territory. Third, her parents' anger makes Laura feel sad and worthless. Unfortunately, her favorite pick-me-up is the activity that gets her into trouble in the first place.

There's a better way to eliminate Laura's and other children's misadventures—a method that doesn't involve anger, lectures, or physical force. The time-out approach, which has long been touted by child rearing experts as the most humane means of shaping a child's behavior, imposes limits instead of punishment and encourages self-control rather than self-loathing. The time-out approach is inherently simple. It's also amazingly effective when used correctly.

Therein lies the problem. You've probably had occasion to witness frazzled parents dangling time-out as a threat, or using the approach in the heat of anger. You may also have seen time-outs devoted to arguments or long-winded lectures. Wrong, wrong, and wrong again! A true time-out isn't a catch-all punishment or a provision for a captive audience. It's a way to promote your child's compliance with specific rules of behavior. The keys to making time-out work are patience, consistency, and knowledge of the technique's finer points. You'll need to tap your personal resolve for the first two ingredients; this book can provide the third.

Time-Out for Children is written with today's adults in mind. You're committed to rearing happy, stable children, and you actively seek professional advice on doing so. The paradox? Your schedule affords you less time than ever before to ponder expert theory and pore over research. This book, with its concise text, case histories, lists, and step-by-step instructions, presents important information in a manner that's both easy and fascinating to read. Parents, caregivers, and teachers can use *Time-Out for Children* as a ready reference in times of discipline crisis, or to prepare for behavioral situations yet to come. In addition, you can use its chapters for applying time-out to older children, your youngster's behavior away from home, and sibling or playmate conflicts. Most important, you can use the book to affirm that your encouragement of your child's good behavior is right on target.

By absorbing the information and following the steps presented in this book, you'll remove emotion from the act of disciplining your child. In doing so, you'll discover how to set limits without power struggles, blowups, and ego-damaging commentaries.

Life in our society is shaped by rules, but compliance is a learned skill. Whether your child is two years old or ten, *Time-Out for Children* will give her, rather than the adults in her life, the responsibility for mastering the necessary lessons.

A Word About Gender

Your child is certainly as likely to be a boy as a girl; however, our language does not provide us with a genderless pronoun. To avoid using the awkward "he/she" when referring to your child, while still giving equal time to both sexes, the masculine pronouns "he," "him," and "his" have been used in odd-numbered chapters, while the female "she," "her," and "hers" appear in all the rest. This decision was made in the interest of simplicity and clarity.

Introduction

"Whenever my son gets angry, he bites someone."

"My daughter talks back every time I correct her."

"My children are constantly at war."

"Nothing I do seems to help!"

Until now, that is. If your child is like the millions of others who habitually act out when angered or stressed, *Time-Out for Children* may provide the answer to your frustration. The time-out approach—that is, briefly, matter-of-factly isolating your child following a predeter-

1

mined offense—is the only discipline tactic that
gives your youngster, not her parent, teacher, or
caregiver, the responsibility for behaving in a
socially appropriate manner. One caveat, however: the mechanics of the time-out technique
are critical to its success.

Use time-out sporadically, in anger, or with
well-meant lectures, and you'll render the
approach ineffective. You see, the parental
detachment and repetition that make the technique different from standard discipline methods are at the core of its success. Fortunately,
Time-Out for Children can serve as your how-to
manual. Within the pages of this book, you'll
find all the information and examples you'll
ever need to shape your child's behavior with
time-out.

Are you confused as to why time-out
works better than punishment or scolding?
Chapter One explains the benefits of the technique, as well as the secrets to its success. Also
included is information on why "getting in
trouble" fails to deter misbehavior. The partic-
ulars of time-out—when, where, for how long,
and for whom to use the approach—are
spelled out in Chapter Two, along with details
to help you refine your technique. Chapter
Three takes you and your child through every

step of the time-out process and spells out the importance of marking the beginning and end with a portable timer. It also offers trouble-shooting tips, in case your initial efforts are unsuccessful.

Time-out in public places is discussed in Chapter Four, with information on how to apply the approach when you're visiting, shopping, dining out, or touring a public attraction. You'll learn the pitfalls of public time-out and find out how not to invite nega-tive behavior when you and your child are out and about. Of course, misbehavior is hardly confined to the preschool set. Chapter Five covers the use of time-out with children from six to ten years of age, describing modifica-tions that keep the technique working. Other discipline tactics for older children are also dis-cussed, along with strategies for handling the rebellious.

Chapter Six, on time-out in the classroom, is useful to parents and teachers alike. Strategies are presented for heading off behavior prob-lems, disarming attention-getters, and becom-ing a more effective communicator. Step-by-step instructions are provided for using time-out at school. In Chapter Seven, variations of the time-out approach are explored. You'll learn when to use these alternative tactics, why they work, and when to draw the line between everyday squabbles and fighting. The final chapter, Chapter Eight, promotes the encouragement of your child's desirable behavior. Information is presented on avoiding behavioral pitfalls, boosting self-esteem, and using tangible rewards to reinforce your youngster's most appropriate words and deeds.

Each chapter is rich with anecdotes, lists, and charts to make the text interesting to read and easy to absorb. And, for parents who want more information on the topic of discipline, a suggested reading list has been included.

Self-control is at the heart of acceptable social behavior. You'll assist your child in developing this crucial trait every time you attach the negative consequence of time-out to an outburst or misdeed. More effective than scolding, more humane than punishment, the time-out technique enables your child to be in full charge of her conduct. Time-out is a loving discipline, and as such, is the right path for parents to choose. Good luck!

1
The Ground Rules

Two-year-old Jesse is a screamer. The youngest child of parents in their forties, he learned early on that the quickest way to have his needs met was to announce them—as shrilly and frantically as possible. Jesse's sisters, ages eleven and thirteen, dote on their little brother. His parents tend to give in to the boy as well, freely admitting that they lack the energy to deal with his prickliness. When Jesse's shrieks become too much to bear, they try a combination of approaches—yelling, hand-slapping, banishing the boy to his crib—all of which only serve to frustrate the child further. Jesse's parents feel that there's lit-

tle chance for good behavior unless they first resolve the matter of their son's screaming.

In counseling, Jesse's parents were advised to respond matter-of-factly, rather than angrily, to their son's screaming, and use a two-minute time-out as a consequence. They, in turn, explained the method to Jesse's sisters and caregiver. With a portable timer in control of the boy's isolation periods, his usual tantrums lost their effectiveness. By the end of only one day of time-outs, Jesse had already figured out that calming himself was the quickest way back to his toys.

Chapter One explains why the time-out technique works so well—with Jesse and with children of all ages. You'll understand the importance of reserving emotion for your child's appropriate behavior and learn the secrets to using the time-out approach effectively. Little Jesse still lets out an occasional screech when he's frustrated, but the time-out technique has sent this two-year-old a long way down the path to self-control. Read on to reap the same benefits for your child.

Time-out is a discipline tactic that employs social techniques to shape a child's behavior. Since children learn much of their behavior through observing others—and the rest from the consequences of their misdeeds—the way you discipline has a clear and lasting effect on your child's social and emotional development. Time-out's simple, direct feedback enables your child to focus on his actions rather than on the intensity of your response.

The crux of the time-out concept is isolation—that is, a brief banishment to a nonstimulating site following a particular action behavior. This isolation is much like the exclusion an adult might face after acting inappropriately. To us, the potential for financial, career, or social penalty is an effective deterrent to offensive words or deeds. The time-out approach encourages a child to toe the line of social acceptance in a similar fashion.

No matter what you call your child's isolation periods, and no matter where they take place, the effect is the same. First, you both get an opportunity to calm down. Second, your child has a chance to ponder his misbehavior. Third, he is reminded that there are social consequences to doing wrong. And last, he is able to move beyond the infraction immediately after paying his dues.

TIME-OUT VS.
"GETTING IN TROUBLE"

Traditional methods of discipline—ultima-
tums, yelling, spankings, and guilt—don't
make the grade with many of today's parents,
caregivers, and teachers. Most know the
importance of self-esteem, and realize how
damaging harshness and physical punishment
can be. While today's discipline methods are
often milder, however, it's still quite common
for parents to view their children's wrongdoings as deliberately provocative, rather than as
an expression of frustration or a bid for help.

When children "get in trouble"—or more
accurately, get attention following a wrongdoing—little is done to change the inappropriate
behavior. Worse, nothing happens to reinforce
what is right. In fact, this condition usually causes the negative conduct to escalate. Time-out, a
positive approach that incorporates setting limits and praising good behavior, has been shown
to be more effective at teaching self-control.

Why is time-out so effective at shaping a
child's behavior? Because, devoid of emotional
repercussions, the technique leaves the child's
self-esteem intact in a way that no other form of
discipline can. Simply and matter-of-factly,

behavior problems are dealt with at the moment they occur, and this prevents the situation—and adult frustration—from escalating. Marking the minutes spent in isolation with a portable timer eliminates parent/child conflict over the control of the time-out session. Most important, a few minutes in isolation enables the child to:

- Reestablish self-control.
- Clearly understand which behavior needs to change.
- See a cause-and-effect relationship between his misdeed and its result.
- Extinguish the target behavior through repetition and practice.
- Remain secure in his loving relationship with the adult in charge.
- Earn immediate forgiveness.

Time-out works because it extinguishes undesirable behavior in a way that leaves the child feeling renewed and responsible for his actions. If he follows household rules, he is free to pursue his usual routine. If he acts out, there's a swift but brief loss of freedom to remind him that it's unacceptable to infringe on the rights or property of others. When he's finished with time-out, he resumes his activities without recrimination or angry feelings.

WHAT ARE THE KEYS TO USING TIME-OUT?

Self-involvement may be a dominant trait among children, but the time-out method will help teach your youngster that his behavior has an impact on those around him. As with any child-rearing technique, it helps to consider the how's and why's before first using the approach. The following ground rules will make your child's time-outs more effective.

■ *Require consistency among the adults in charge of your child.* For the time-out technique to work, your child needs to know that rules—and the consequences of breaking them—are constant. Asking your child's caregivers to respond as you do to misbehavior eliminates confusion and ultimately, is less stressful for all concerned.

■ *Target only one or two misbehaviors at a time.* Declaring time-out for every infraction may lead to hours spent in isolation each day. Instead, help your child understand the link

THE BENEFITS OF TIME-OUT

The time-out approach is superior to other discipline techniques because:

- ■ It clarifies which behavior is inappropriate.
- ■ It leaves the child's self-esteem intact.
- ■ It addresses misbehavior instantly.
- ■ It minimizes power struggles.
- ■ It allows the child to continue to feel loved.
- ■ It makes the child responsible for his actions.

between misbehavior and penalty by reserving time-out for particular wrongdoings. When that behavior is eliminated, you can target something else.

■ *Employ time-out immediately.* The connection between misbehavior and isolation is clearest when the consequence is enforced without prior warnings, debate, or delay. Declaring time-out swiftly removes the possibility of compromise and leaves your child no time for stubbornness or attempts at manipulation.

■ *Assign time-out without anger.* The time-out technique was developed as a positive means of shaping a child's behavior, and your businesslike demeanor is what keeps it so. Voicing annoyance or using bodily force to get your child to the time-out spot makes the approach punitive and puts you back in control of your child's behavior.

■ *Don't belabor the point.* Lecturing your child while he's in time-out invites denial and debate that takes away his chance to calmly reflect on the circumstances that got him there. Chastising him afterward minimizes the fact that your child has paid his dues and makes him resentful, thereby erasing his pleasure in having regained self-control.

■ *Balance time-outs with reinforcement of good behavior.* To increase the effectiveness of time-out, it pays to give your child's good behavior the amount of attention formerly paid to his wrongdoings. Rewarding your youngster's special efforts with smiles, praise, and

KEYS TO TIME-OUT SUCCESS

Here are the secrets to maximizing the effectiveness of time-out:

■ Consistency among caregivers.

■ Careful selection of target behaviors.

■ Immediate use after infractions.

■ Separating emotion from discipline.

■ Reinforcement of good behavior.

physical affection will make the minutes spent in time-out less appealing than ever.

Will your child be happy about your switch to the time-out approach? Not at first, and here's why: By isolating your young offender in a businesslike fashion, you leave no room for emotion-charged apologies, tantrums, or angry debate—the kinds of interactions that used to secure your attention and take the spotlight off your child's misdeed. His unhappiness about time-out will be short-lived, however, once he realizes that he's in charge of ending his isolation periods and avoiding repeat performances. The beauty of the time-out approach is that is helps your child to govern his own behavior—eliminating the power struggles of old and laying the foundation for self-control.

SIMPLE ENOUGH FOR A TODDLER TO USE

"Kyra was playing with an alligator push toy when all of a sudden, she went running to the kitchen and came back empty-handed. 'I'm giving my alligator a time-out,' she announced, 'because he no listen to me.' (She was barely two at the time.) She went running back to get the toy only to return it to the kitchen a few minutes later. 'He's getting another time-out. He *still* no listen.'"

Lisa Rudolph
Correspondent, Dateline NBC

2

The Particulars of the Technique

William, age five, was banished to his room up to a dozen times a day for hitting. When angered, he would pummel his brother, smack his friends, and even deliver a swat to Mom or Dad. Once in his room, however, William would throw a tantrum of such proportions that his parents would rush in to stop him from hurting himself. Of course, each response of this type ensured that subsequent banishments would bring even more vigorous kicking and head-banging.

It was suggested that William's parents plan their son's time-outs for a safe and visible, but

*utterly boring location — the living room couch.
When they employed a portable timer and a hard-
and-fast rule about waiting to set it till William was
quiet, the boy's tantrums became a thing of the past.
Though he howled and thrashed for a full thirty-six
minutes the first time, the next three time-outs
brought tantrums of four minutes, one minute, and
fifteen seconds in length. Ever since, William has
accepted time-outs with resignation rather than
hysteria.*

*Chapter Two provides the details of the time-out
approach. You'll learn when and where to stage
your child's time-outs, how long they should last,
and for whom the technique works. You'll also be
given guidelines for boosting time-out's effectiveness. Through time-out, young William is learning
to tame his aggression and temper. This chapter
provides the background you'll need to make similar
strides with your child.*

What makes the time-out technique yield rapid results in one household but fail to work at all in another? The secret lies in paying attention to the finer points of the approach—your timing, the chosen location, and the duration of your time-out periods. Also important is the age of the child in question. By plotting your strategy ahead of time, you'll be ready to assign time-outs that work.

WHO BENEFITS FROM THE TIME-OUT APPROACH?

Time-out works to curb inappropriate behavior in children of all ages. Among the younger set—that is, two- to five-year-olds—the method is particularly effective against common aggressive impulses. Time-out imposes a restraint that preschool children find very hard to tolerate. Therefore, behaviors such as biting, hitting, and hair-pulling vanish within a matter of days when each outburst is met with the same businesslike response.

As your child grows and becomes increasingly socialized, chronic behavior problems are more likely to center on interactions with peers, siblings, and adults in charge. "Telling" is common among six- to nine-year-olds, as are talking back and fighting. To children in this age group, time-out is an interruption—and an incredibly boring one, at that. The displeasing prospect of isolation encourages conversation, cooperation, and self-reliance.

TIME-OUT FOR WHOM?

The time-out approach is not appropriate for children under two or over twelve, or for the types of behaviors described on page 90. However, this approach to discipline can work wonders with children who are:

Two to twelve years of age.

Disruptive or impulsive.

Hard to get along with.

Aggressive.

Argumentative or rude.

Inclined toward foul language.

Much of your older child's behavior is best shaped by logical consequences—say, revoking bicycle privileges for careless riding, or confiscating a video game that has siblings at war. Among ten- to twelve-year-olds, however, there are certain social misbehaviors for which no logical consequence exists. Rudeness, for instance, or foul language, or lying cannot be responded to in kind, no matter what the circumstances. When time-out is the consequence, however, impulses of this type are quickly controlled. Preteenagers tend to be impatient with—and somewhat embarrassed by—discipline measures that cramp their social style.

WHEN SHOULD TIME-OUT BE ASSIGNED?

You can begin employing the time-out method when you have targeted one or two of your child's behaviors that you wish to change. For the time-out approach to be immediately effective, the target misdeed(s) should be something that is "countable"—that is, clear-cut and unmistakable—and occurs more than once a day. It's important to spell out to your child which behavior merits a time-out. You should

WHAT *NOT* TO DO (OR SAY)

The time-out approach is inherently simple—but it's easy to use the technique incorrectly. The following words and deeds will undermine your efforts to change your child's behavior and should be avoided.

■ Don't say, "For *that* *y*ou're going to time-out!" The technique is meant to teach acceptable behavior, not punish wrongdoing.

■ Don't calm your child if she has a tantrum during time-out. Attention of any type makes fussing worthwhile.

■ Don't say, "If you do that one more time. . . ." It's most effective to declare time-out after a *first* infraction..

■ Don't demand an apology for misbehavior. After a time-out, your child may feel embarrassed or misunderstood. There's no point in "rubbing it in."

■ Don't say, "I hate to do this. . . . ," or "I'm sorry, but . . . . " when placing your child in time-out. Apologies weaken your position.

■ Don't apply the technique without first defining target behaviors. Putting your child in time-out for every infraction is too disruptive.

If you keep these guidelines in mind, the time-out approach will be less upsetting to you and your child—and more effective at reducing undesirable behavior.

also explain, and even practice, the technique beforehand.

It's advisable to target a smaller problem behavior at first—say, teasing a younger sibling, rather than hitting or biting. This way, the initial exposure to time-out takes place when your child is in a calm, unemotional state of mind. The more receptive your youngster feels when isolated, the quicker she'll be to gain control over inappropriate impulses.

Optimally, time-out should be declared within ten seconds of the time you observe or hear your child breaking the pre-discussed rule. This stops the misbehavior before it has a chance to escalate into something unmanageable. It also leaves no room for responses like, "What did I do?" and "No, I didn't!".

WHERE SHOULD TIME-OUT TAKE PLACE?

The ideal location for time-out is away from people, toys, television, and other distractions. Anything that makes your child's isolation periods more tolerable only reduces their effectiveness. It's important that you select a place that is safe, that is nonthreatening, and that can be easily supervised by the adult in charge. A hallway or corner of a room is a good choice.

It helps to provide a chair for use during time-out. Doing so helps create specific boundaries for the isolated child and prevents rolling and other full-body distractions. If your older child needs less direct supervision and is embarrassed by banishment to a corner or hallway, time-out can take place at the dining room table, or in the guest room, the study, or a similar quiet location.

MAKING TIME-OUT BORING

To make time-out as little fun as possible, separate your child from the following distractions:

- Siblings and friends.
- Noise from radio or television.
- Pets.
- Toys and books.
- Windows.
- Knickknacks.

The same guidelines apply when you need to declare time-out away from home (see Chapter Four). Any out-of-the-way place that separates your child from the people and activities at hand will work well.

TIME-OUT, OR TIME TO READ?

"My daughter is a bookworm. She would read crossing the street if I let her. Should I find the need to give her some reflective time-out, it only serves to increase her reading time. While she resents being told where to go, unless I build a book-free dungeon, she really doesn't mind being told to 'go to your room!'"

Jack Bierman
Editor-in-Chief,
L.A. Parent magazine

HOW LONG SHOULD TIME-OUTS LAST?

Research shows that time-out is most effective when its duration is linked to the child's age. After all, a child's tolerance level increases as she gets older. A good rule of thumb is to assign one minute of isolation for each year of your child's age. This returns preschoolers to their activities after just two or three minutes, while banishing older children for somewhat longer.

At first, it's best to demand just thirty seconds of quiet. A portable timer is the best way to mark the passage of time, because doing so helps separate the adult in charge from the discipline process. Use of a timer pits child against clock rather than child against adult. It also gives your child control over another aspect of her time-outs—when to leave.

Refusing to set the timer until your child sits quietly lays the groundwork for a power struggle that undermines the effectiveness of time-out. Instead, you may wish to add an additional thirty seconds if your child is still noisy when the timer rings to signal the end of time-out. She'll quickly realize that she controls her exit. Once she grasps the idea, you can begin to lengthen her time-outs by fifteen-second increments until they're the recommended length.

The time-out method can reduce the incidence of inappropriate behavior in children of all ages. The location and duration of your child's banishment may vary over the years, but with periodic reassessment and minor changes, the approach will continue to work its disciplinary magic.

3
Making it Work

Four-year-old Katey is the only child of a couple who describe their own upbringings as "incredibly strict." Because spanking and punishment was a large factor in their early lives, Katey's parents find the matter of discipline to be quite unpleasant. They avoid setting rules and tend to look the other way or call out a reminder when their child does something wrong. Sometimes, they try to cajole her into behaving with a "Be a good girl, now." Katey senses her parents' ambivalence and has learned that there are few controls over her behavior—and almost no consequences. As a result, she is becoming rude and very wild.

It was suggested that Katey's parents begin establishing their authority through the time-out approach. Katey's mother hesitated at first, because she felt the technique might be too time-consuming for a working couple. She did not wish to devote the family's night and weekend time to discipline. However, Katey responded immediately to the approach, in large part because of her parents' customary even-temperedness. At first, time-out was used to minimize Katey's aggressiveness. When the little girl showed a new ability to calm herself after less than two weeks, her parents decided to extend time-out to instances of rudeness. The technique was again successful.

Chapter Three presents step-by-step instructions for applying the time-out method to two-through five-year-olds. You'll learn exactly what to say and do to assign, oversee, and end time-outs with gentle authority. In addition, suggestions are included for handling common time-out problems. Thanks to the time-out approach, little Katey is becoming more responsive to the rights and feelings of others. The information in this chapter can pave the way for similar improvements in your child's behavior.

When time-out is the consequence of a wrong-doing, your child understands at once that his behavior is unacceptable and that he now has an opportunity to calm down and start over. As stressed in previous chapters, the approach works best when used calmly and unfailingly.

GETTING READY TO USE TIME-OUT

For the time-out technique to be effective in eliminating problem behavior, it's important to follow a series of prescribed steps. If your child is older than three years of age, you may find it very helpful to involve him or her in the setup of your household's time-outs. The steps you should take are listed below.

Lay the Groundwork

Explain to your child that he will now be in charge of following family rules against the target misbehavior. It helps to stress that you love him and want to help him act appropriately by giving him a chance to sit and think each time he breaks the rule. Tell your child that his thinking breaks will be called time-outs and that they'll be governed by a timer. Show him where his time-outs will take place.

Establish Rules

Discuss putting an end to yelling and arguing about behavior since time-outs will be spent in silence. Talk with your child about how long it might take him to reflect on rulebreaking. Older children may want some input, but remember, your goal is one minute per year of your child's age. Discuss what the adult in charge will be doing while time-out is in progress. Also, explain that a timer is in charge of ending time-outs.

Decide on a Target Behavior

Talk to your child about behaviors that cause problems for him and others. Choose something that occurs several times a day, and discuss the importance of erasing that particular behavior. Explain that from now on, time-out will be the consequence of that wrongdoing.

Gather Your Props

Select an appropriate location for time-outs to take place. (See page 22 for details.) Remove distractions, put a chair in place and get a portable timer, such as Sanitoy, Inc.'s "Tommy the Time-Out Teacher." You'll want to position the timer nearby when time-out is in progress so your child can hear it ring.

Do a Dry Run

Tell your child that you're going to have a "practice" time-out. Ask him to pretend that he has
just exhibited the target behavior. Immediately
name the infraction and the consequence, as in,
"Hitting is not allowed. Go to time-out *now*."
Lead your child to the designated chair in silence,

WHY A TIMER?

Why not keep track of time-outs with a wrist-
watch or oven timer? Because a portable timer:

- Takes the onus off you as "the bad guy."
- Eliminates pleading for an early end to time-out.
- Relieves you of clock-watching.
- Eliminates the risk that you'll forget to retrieve your child.
- Reminds siblings and others to keep away.
- Gives your child responsibility for rejoining the household at the proper time.

set the timer for a few seconds, and walk away. When the timer goes off, remind him that he may now leave the chair. In this instance only, congratulate him for following the rules of time-out.

Be Aware of Words and Deeds That Warrant Praise

Being isolated after misbehavior is a negative consequence. Paying attention to your child's

---

STEP BY STEP

Once you and your child understand the time-out approach, the technique itself is quite simple. The steps involved are listed below in brief.

1. Look for the target behavior.

2. Name the behavior and call a time-out.

3. Direct your child to the time-out spot.

4. Set the timer.

5. Remove the timer when it rings.

good behavior while actively ignoring the bad teaches social appropriateness and increases the likelihood that he'll conduct himself properly in the future. In addition, praise builds self-esteem and promotes good feelings between parent and child.

Watch for the Target Misbehavior

It's important to react immediately, so there's no room for your child to forget or deny the infraction. Another key to success is catching every occurrence of the misbehavior. This may require close scrutiny at first, but with proper use of time-out, the behavior will diminish almost at once.

Declare a Time-Out

In as few words as possible, tell your child that he has done wrong and, as you discussed earlier, must now serve a time-out. Use a mild, businesslike tone of voice and point or lead your child to the time-out place as you speak. Avoid yelling, scolding, or lecturing.

Set the Timer

The time to be spent in isolation should equal one minute per year of your child's age. For example,

"WHAT SHOULD
I DO IF . . . ?"

If the time-out technique doesn't seem to work for you, don't despair! Often, all that's needed is a closer look at how—and when—you put the approach to use. Here are some common time-out problems and solutions.

My child will not stay in time-out.

■ Carry or lead your child back to time-out, calmly resetting the timer in each case.

■ Sit in the time-out chair yourself, holding your child on your lap. Start the timer when your child stops struggling.

My older child refuses to go to time-out.

■ Calmly repeat your command and tack on an extra minute for each delay.

■ After three minutes of delays, cancel a privilege. (Time-out must still be served.)

My child comes back from time-out and immediately repeats the misbehavior.

■ Before your child resumes playing, ask him why he served a time-out.

■ Look for opportunities to praise your child's good behavior.

My child throws a tantrum whenever he goes to time-out.

■ Assign time-out earlier, before your child has a chance to lose control.

■ Be sure that you assign time-out in a calm, nonpunitive manner.

My child makes a deliberate mess while in time-out.

■ Confiscate misused items and add on minutes for clean-up.

■ Move your child's time-outs to a barren location like the hallway.

Establishing a workable time-out procedure may require some technical adjustments at first. But in the long run, you'll find that the approach requires minimal effort.

---

time-out for a four-year-old should last four minutes. Information on building up to the appropriate interval is given on page 25. Place the timer nearby so your child can hear when it rings.

Remain Silent

Avoid speaking to your child for the duration of time-out. Remember, the time is to be spent in silence, reflecting on what your youngster did wrong. You can stay within visual range or earshot, depending on the age of your child,

THERE'S ALWAYS SOMETHING . . .

"An expert I once interviewed said that children should spend their time-out periods in rooms that were as bare as possible, such a laundry or mud room. So, the next time my five-year-old hit his younger brother, I put him in the laundry room and told him to stay for five minutes until he understood why his action was wrong. Two minutes later, I heard a crash and walked into the laundry room to find my detergent cup on the floor and my son standing on top of the washing machine reaching for the action figure I'd stashed on a shelf after finding it in a pants pocket. Can any room be neutral enough for a curious child?"

Roberta Israeloff
Writer, author, and contributing editor at Parents magazine

but it's important to make it obvious that your attention is turned elsewhere.

Remove the Timer

When the bell rings to signal the end of time-out, put the timer out of sight without saying a word. If your child remains seated, you can calmly remind him that time-out is over and he can now resume playing. Ask why he was sent to time-out, and don't mention the incident again.

If you yell at a misbehaving child, you'll convince him that the way to handle conflict is to instill fear. If you toss out warnings instead, you'll convey that it's acceptable to ignore your first requests. Only the time-out approach provides the kind of instant, nonpunitive feedback that encourages a child to take charge of his behavior.

4
Public
Places

Three-year-old Raymond's parents avoided taking their son out in public because of his willful, demanding behavior. At home, rules of conduct were carefully enforced, but in front of others, Raymond's parents tended to relinquish control. Private people, they hesitated to create a scene and feared that disciplining the boy in a store or restaurant would hold their parenting skills up to public scrutiny. When pressed, Raymond's father admitted that he avoided taking a stand when out with his son because he'd look foolish if the boy refused to listen. Over time, the couple's hesitancy convinced

*their child that he was in control when other people
were around. Wherever the family went, Raymond's
parents could count on their son creating a ruckus.*

*A counselor helped Raymond's parents evaluate
the situation by asking them to compare their at-
home and in-public modes of discipline. The couple
saw their inconsistency at once, and quickly understood that their son's public misbehavior was the
result of their ignoring his earlier antics. Once they
steeled themselves to ignore the curious glances of
onlookers, Raymond's parents began to respond to
their boy's away-from-home conduct with time-
outs — as swiftly and surely as they did in private.
When Raymond realized that behavior rules would
now be enforced regardless of time or place, he
stopped his demands and tantrums almost at once.*

*Chapter Four describes how to use the time-out
approach when you and your child are away from
home. Guidelines for minimizing incidences of misbehavior are included, as are techniques for handling infractions that do occur — whether at friends'
homes, at outdoor events, or in stores, restaurants,
or other public buildings. Little Raymond became
more compliant when he learned that time-outs
could take place almost anywhere. By learning to
apply this discipline tactic in public, you'll be able
to effect the same kind of improvement in your
child's conduct.*

I t's far simpler to discipline your child in the privacy of your home than it is to do so when others are watching. Responding to public misconduct is a measure of your skill as a parent that carries the potential for embarrassment. What if your child answers back or refuses to cooperate with the consequences you set? You'll appear ineffective, that's what—and this knowledge leads many parents to overlook behavior in public that would never be tolerated at home. Just as with Raymond, though, a child who perceives that household rules don't apply to public places can be counted on to flaunt this newfound power. To make appropriate behavior a constant with your child, it's vital to use the same discipline approach in a museum, shop, or friend's house that you use at home. Away-from-home time-outs are as effective at eliminating misconduct as enforced isolation in a hallway or foyer.

THE PITFALLS OF PUBLIC TIME-OUT

The presence of onlookers does more than make you conscious of your effectiveness as a parent. Whether they are friends or strangers, other people form an arena that tends to magnify behavioral aberrations, because your child's public conduct—and your ability to control it—says a lot about who is in charge. Using time-out in public presents special challenges, as outlined below.

■ *Onlookers.* No matter how occasional her misbehavior may be, the child who acts rude or whiny in public reflects badly on the supervising parent. Your discomfiture can easily compel you to nag, fuss, or explode at your youngster's misconduct.

■ *The humiliation factor.* Discipline that's enacted in a public place can be embarrassing to a child. Parents can inadvertently make things worse by employing a tone of voice or invoking a consequence that calls additional attention to the situation.

■ *Lack of facilities.* At home, a designated chair or stairway landing makes a perfect place for temporary exile. But when you are guests, customers, or patrons, finding a corner that's boring enough—and safe enough—for timing-out a rambunctious child can call for a bit of creativity. A public phone alcove or an empty restaurant booth are two possibilities.

■ *The duration question.* Invoking a public time-out is a challenge in itself. In a makeshift location and under the watchful gaze of others, seeing the consequence completely through may be all but impossible.

It is worth trying to overcome these challenges, however, because time-out works only when it is the immediate consequence of misbehavior.

THE TROUBLE WITH DELAYED TIME-OUTS

What if your child acts out in a house of worship, in the middle of a celebratory dinner, or during a bus ride? Tempted though you may be to schedule a time-out for later on, you'll find this practice less effective, and much more difficult to enforce, than immediate isolation. Here are the problems with delayed time-outs:

■ A time-out served well after an infraction makes the approach feel punitive.

■ You give your child time to formulate an argument.

■ Your child may forget the details—or the occurrence—of her misdeed.

■ You may forget to follow through or, in

MANAGEMENT TIPS
FOR PUBLIC TIME-OUTS

Here are the keys to effective use of time-out in a public place.

■ *Accentuate the positive.* Remember to praise behavior that is appropriate.

■ *Ignore onlookers.* A few curious stares may be the price of consistent discipline.

■ *Be prepared.* Select a boring time-out spot as soon as you arrive at your destination.

■ *Make time-outs safe.* Because children need ongoing supervision, be sure to keep your youngster in your field of vision at all times.

the face of more appropriate behavior, be tempted to overlook the scheduled time-out.

Remember, time-out is based on the premise that certain infractions have an immediate consequence. Delay that consequence, and you've taken away the cause/effect deterrent to unacceptable conduct. Removing your child from church or temple, excusing yourselves from the dining room, or isolating the youngster in an empty bus seat are certainly inconveniences. When you do so, however, your child will quickly realize that behavior rules are to be taken seriously.

The keys to making time-out work in public places are planning ahead and patterning your public discipline technique after the approach you use at home. You'll find your child's public time-outs to be effective and relatively comfortable for all concerned if you earmark a time-out site at the start of your visit, adopt a purposeful, businesslike air, take pains to use an even tone of voice, and reduce the length of your child's isolation by about a third. Naturally, your child won't like interrupting a visit, meal, or excursion for a time-out, but when she learns that acting up in public carries a sure consequence, she'll work harder at maintaining self-control.

TIME-OUT WHILE VISITING

Lasting impressions aside, the biggest problem with misbehavior while a guest in someone's home is the potential for destruction and danger. Your house may be child-safe and subject to preset rules, but that doesn't mean your youngster won't run wild amid Aunt Joan's antiques or target a two-year-old cousin for a few karate moves. Once the time-out approach is well established at home, it's a simple matter to extend it to the homes of others.

■ Prepare your child for the day's events. Discuss behavior and explain that time-out will be in use during your visit. Pack your timer.

■ Plan to keep your youngster busy with toys and a generous dose of adult attention.

■ Explain your discipline policy to your host and ask permission to designate a time-out area. If you sense that your host might intrude, consider using the front steps, the lobby, or your car, as appropriate. Of course, the location you choose should enable your child to remain under your watchful eye.

■ Isolate your child at the first infraction. In the interest of company manners, keep her in time-out for only half of the normal time period.

You'll find that time-out while visiting is extremely effective, because interrupting play at a friend's or relative's house is just as annoying to a child as doing so at home.

A *REAL* ROADSIDE TIME-OUT

"I came across the following very effective trick in a magazine. When my children start acting up on local car trips (which happens often, since we live on a country road and have to drive miles to get anywhere), I pull over, order the kids out of the car, drive ahead as far as I can without losing sight of them, shut off the car, and wait. By the time they reach me, I'm calm and they're ready to behave themselves.'"

Allison R., mother of two
Via the Internet

TIME-OUT ON THE ROAD

The close quarters enforced by car travel create numerous possibilities for misbehavior. Using the time-out technique requires patience on the part of all family members, but the result can be swift and dramatic. Here's what to do.

1. Before leaving, spell out your travel plans and the behavior you expect from your child. Be clear about the consequences of misconduct, and ask the temporary indulgence of other family members.

2. Appreciate how boring car travel can be. Pack activities and snacks, and provide adult company by occasionally rotating seats.

3. Pull off the road when time-out is necessary. Tell your child why she's being disciplined.

4. On short trips, remove your child from the car and have her stand in the L formed by the passenger door and sideview mirror. On long trips, park your vehicle and have your child remain inside for time-out while the rest of the family stretches their legs. Stay within sight of your child, of course.

You may wonder whether time-out on the road will play havoc with your itinerary, but repetition is usually unnecessary. Your child is probably more eager to reach your destination than you are.

TIME-OUT IN PUBLIC BUILDINGS

Shopping, touring, and dining out provide the key components of behavioral disaster: a distracted adult and an easily bored child. Keeping your youngster's natural limits in mind when planning your outing can help you avoid many difficult situations, but sometimes, misbehavior happens anyway. Here's what to do.

■ En route, describe your child's role in your outing. Mention that you've brought along your timer, and specify behavior(s) that will trigger time-out.

■ Choose an isolation area. An empty restaurant table, a corner of a store, or a museum or mall bench are perfect for time-out, as long as your child stays within view. If your child is being extremely disruptive, you may wish to distance yourselves from others by going outdoors or to your car.

■ Cut the usual duration of time-outs in half. This makes an uncomfortable situation seem less so for everyone.

Initially, you may dislike using time-out in a public place, but other parents will understand exactly what you're doing. In addition, you're likely to need the time-out technique only rarely. Your child won't like public discipline any more than you do.

"YOU'RE ASKING FOR TROUBLE IF . . ."

It's all too easy to invite misbehavior when you and your child are out in public. You'll head off many embarrassing moments by avoiding the following traps.

■ *Failing to prepare your child for an outing.* You'll elicit better behavior if you share your agenda and lay down the rules ahead of time.

■ *Making an overly long social call.* Even if your destination includes playmates, two to three hours is all the "company behavior" most children can muster.

■ *Running errands that offer nothing for your child to do.* A bored youngster will either look to you for amusement or create some diversion of her own.

■ *Expecting behavior that isn't required at home.* You can't expect Johnny to stay seated at a restaurant table if he is permitted to wander when dining at home.

■ *Neglecting to closely monitor your child's behavior.* If they are dealt with immediately, little problems won't escalate to the blowup stage.

■ *Forgetting to offer positive attention.* Friends and activities won't entirely substitute for feedback from Mom and Dad.

With forethought, preparation, and consideration of your child's needs, your family's outings will be more enjoyable for all.

TIME-OUT AT OUTDOOR FUNCTIONS

Encouraging self-control at a park, pool, or playground is as important as doing so indoors. The combination of open space and an atmosphere of fun tends to dispel inhibition, thereby setting the stage for exuberant or aggressive behavior. Time-out is a great device for keeping things under control.

■ Make your behavioral expectations clear beforehand.

■ Remind your child that you have brought the timer along.

■ At your destination, earmark a safe, easily monitored time-out zone.

■ If your child misbehaves, call time-out immediately.

■ Set the timer for half of the usual time and put your child in control of her return to play.

Your child may find the isolation tactic to be particularly distasteful amid crowds and out-door fun. You can help her to remain aware of the time-out consequence—and therefore, keep her behavior in check—by being the one to choose its location. As with other public places, you're not likely to need the approach too often.

5
Time-Out and Older Kids

Janice, age eight, seems to be outgrowing her mother's discipline methods. Ever since toddlerhood, disapproving looks and words have been the perfect way to keep the child's behavior in check. Lately, though, the third grader seems to care less about her mother's opinion than about amusing friends with attempts to "buck the system." Janice is becoming disrespectful and fresh, and her mother, who has sole custody, worries that she has lost control of the situation. She is anxious to reestablish behavior rules and restore her daughter's former level of compliance.

Janice's teacher suggested that the mother begin using a modified time-out approach—specifically, banishing the child to the dining room for eight minutes each time she flouted authority. If Janice refused to go, or left the dining room before her time was up, her mother should extend the time-out—but only once. If the girl still didn't comply, there should be no play time, TV, or contact with friends until her time had been served. The teacher felt that with no way to avoid the price of misbehavior, sociable Janice would willingly toe the line.

Chapter Five examines the feasibility of using time-out with children over age five. You'll see why it's necessary to modify the traditional technique as your child grows older, and learn the how's and why's behind some tried-and-true alternatives to isolation. In addition, you'll find out which misbehaviors respond to modified time-out, and what steps to take if your child rebels. When Janice's mother began declaring time-outs, the girl quickly learned that curbing her insubordinate side was much easier than "wasting play time at an empty table." When you vary the time-out approach to suit your child's needs and behavior, you'll be teaching the same lesson.

I f the discipline tactics that you've honed so carefully and applied so consistently during your child's early years begin to lose effectiveness as he moves through elementary school, you'll find yourself with lots of company. The more children expand their horizons, the faster their need for parental approval dwindles in the face of the desire to impress classmates and friends. Often, they may try to do this with episodes of rudeness, teasing, and minor rule-breaking that are as new to them as to their surprised parents. And as misbehavior takes an upswing, the traditional consequence—a time-out—becomes an additional source of conflict. When this happens, it's time to vary your approach to discipline.

WHY IT BECOMES IMPORTANT TO MODIFY TIME-OUT

As your child moves through grade school, he acquires an increasing list of responsibilities. With additional schoolwork, chores, and extra-curricular activities comes increased stress, which can cause your youngster to respond to family discussions and discipline measures with new defiance. You may also notice more manipulative behavior as your child gains awareness of the

PRIME TIMES
FOR TIME-OUT

The time-out approach works particularly well with young children. As your child grows older, however, he is likely to test you with new and different types of misconduct. You'll find that time-out is a very effective deterrent to:

Inappropriate language

Hitting or shoving

Rudeness; backtalk

Cruelty

Screaming

Physically dangerous behavior

Destructiveness

Noncompliance with a command

Because most children over the age of six have begun to develop self control, it follows that your misbehaving older child is provoking you deliberately. Time-out is a great way to nip this tendency in the bud.

feelings of others. Rather than comply peacefully with time-out decrees, he's likely to debate, twist words, and search for loopholes that will turn disciplinary situations to his advantage.

The grade-school years often mean an increase in hours spent away from the family. Left more to his own devices, your child will gain a sense of independence that pleases you both, but plays havoc with the traditional time-out approach. Enforced isolation for misbehavior established you as the guardian of your child's conduct, and this premise may no longer work. Your newly autonomous child will want a say in more than just his departure from time-out. Impulse-control may have been the driving force behind preschool discipline, but your child's good and bad behavior is becoming more deliberate. As such, he may be ready for a larger role in determining and encouraging what is right.

Finally, your growing child is becoming more motivated by popularity. Between ages six and twelve, it is increasingly important to "fit in" among peers, to achieve a social standing in the family, and above all, to save face in sticky situations. Traditional time-out—or, for that matter, any interaction that singles out your child—may become abhorrent. Happily, you can avoid con-

tributing to the social pressures on your child
without relaxing your behavioral standards.

ISSUES FOR PARENTS

Your child isn't the only one affected by the
growing-up process. As a parent, you have to
roll with the punches dealt by your youngster's moody, cocky, or embarrassing behavior. Recollections of your own school years
can serve as proof that later childhood is full
of complications. However, it's also a time
when youngsters need as much parental
guidance as ever. Here's what you may find
yourself struggling with.

■ *The freedom question.* Naturally, you want
to encourage your child's budding independence—however, like most children, he
probably overestimates his own maturity.
It can be a tricky undertaking to grant new
privileges and responsibilities in doses
large enough to make your youngster
happy, but small enough to keep him from
being overwhelmed.

■ *Relinquishing control.* As your child devel-
ops a school and social life of his own, he'll

spend more and more time in the charge of teachers, coaches, and friends' parents. Entrusting your youngster to others, however qualified, is a difficult step. Is there sufficient supervision? Are there behavioral standards that match your own? You can research the conditions and continue to keep a watchful eye on your child, but even so, consistent discipline becomes impossible.

■ *Broadening your focus.* As your youngster struggles to gain a foothold in the grade-school social hierarchy, it often falls to you to protect and bolster his shaky self-image. Praise, hugs, and other positive feedback become all-important, but it can be difficult to step up the congratulations without relaxing your response to incidents of misconduct.

■ *The interest factor.* The modifications made to your discipline approach will only be as effective as your child's feelings about them. The maintenance of the program you choose is a crucial component, but realistically, it is a job that will rest on your shoulders.

To keep your child interested in and unembarrassed by your discipline approach, you'll need to exhibit ongoing enthusiasm.

WAYS TO VARY THE TIME-OUT APPROACH

For some children, traditional time-out remains effective for many years. Many others, however, become immune to the effects of temporary isolation or grow willful enough to

---

TRY THIS

A few simple variations can help the time-out technique remain effective—even with children who have used the approach for years. These suggestions may be helpful.

Instead of . . .

Managing all behavioral issues,

Adding up to five time-out minutes for noncompliance,

Using a traditional time-out,

Briefly stating your child's misdeed ("Time-out for teasing!"),

Leaving it to your child to assimilate increasing responsibilities,

---

resist. Change is needed when ordinary time-out loses its power over your child for any reason. Here are some alternatives.

■ *Revocation of privileges.* If your child shuns time-out, the traditional recommendation is to add time in one-minute incre-

By gradually adapting the time-out technique to your child's maturity level, you can continue for years to help him master the art of self-control.

Try . . .

Setting details down in a parent-child contract.

Grounding your child after the second refusal.

Assigning an extra chore as a consequence.

Being more specific about the problem ("Name-calling is hurtful and cruel.").

Develop a more structured routine at home.

ments. An older child may be unmoved by a longer time-out, or he may become so agitated as the minutes add up that all hope of cooperation is lost. Instead, you may wish to limit additional time to three minutes. If your child still won't comply, you can revoke free-time privileges until the time-out is served.

■ *Assign a penalty task.* As an alternative to time-out, assign a five-minute task that is not part of your family's weekly routine— say, waxing furniture, or wiping out cabinets. If your child doesn't comply, tell him that a second task will be assigned and that he'll be grounded until both jobs are done. As with time-out, do not debate the issue or interact with your child until he is finished.

■ *Take a parental time-out.* When your child is being particularly uncooperative, or when you simply lack the energy to belabor a behavioral issue, you can save face and reduce tension by taking a time-out for yourself. Saying, "—has upset me. I need to cool down before we discuss this," captures your child's attention and reminds him of your position of authority.

IF YOUR CHILD REBELS . . .

At some point, most children decide that "time-out is for babies." If your child thinks he has outgrown the approach, why not try putting him more in control? Here's how.

If your child refuses to go to time-out. . .	*First:* Add one, two, and if necessary, three extra minutes to his isolation period. *If Necessary:* Revoke privileges until time-out has been served.
If your child causes a ruckus in time-out. . .	*First:* Withdraw all attention and move out of sight. *If Necessary:* Add two extra minutes if he is still noisy when the timer rings.

If your child pretends to enjoy time-out. . .	*First:* State that when the timer rings, he can stay or go as he chooses. *If Necessary:* Move to another room until he tires of the waiting game.
If your child leaves time-out too soon. . .	*First:* Add two minutes to his isolation period. *If Necessary:* Revoke privileges until time-out has been served.

It's crucial to stand firm once you've declared a time-out. When your child realizes that he cannot change your mind about isolating him, attempts at rebellion will decrease.

OTHER APPROACHES FOR SIX- TO TWELVE-YEAR OLDS

Reinforcing good conduct is an important step with older children. The approaches described below can help you set standards for good behavior, reward appropriate action, and give your child a pleasing sense of control over your family's discipline process.

■ *A parent/child contract.* When considering a new privilege for your child—say, permission to do homework in his room—it may help to prepare a written agreement. Spell out your child's part of the bargain, and state the consequences of breaking the rules. This approach allows you to pinpoint potential problems and work out solutions.

■ *A school checklist.* This tactic gives your child greater responsibility for his conduct in school. After discussion with the teacher, write the date and desired behavior at the top of an index card. Below that, write fives YESs and NOs for the teacher to circle at the end of each school day. You can award privileges, points, or tokens for every YES your child earns.

■ *A chart system.* You can increase desired behavior by having your child keep visual records. Note the goal behaviors at the top of a chart, and make provisions for daily or weekly assessment, as appropriate. Praise your child's efforts in the short run, and coordinate a reward—say, dimes to put toward a movie ticket—to his daily achievements.

As you work to modify your discipline tactics, your older child will likely be gratified by your efforts. He'll see your flexibility as a sign that you respect his maturity, and he'll enjoy feeling more in charge of his behavior.

PEACE TALKS

Now that my children are older, I time them out as a pair when they fight. They're sent to sit beside one another on the hearth for as long as it takes them to collaborate on a solution to their conflict. When they reach an agreement, I listen, okay their idea, and send them on their way."

Sally Cook
Publisher and Editor,
Central California Parent

6
Time-Out in the Classroom

Nine-year-old Craig started the school year on the right foot. By mid-year, however, he seemed to reach an academic plateau that greatly upset him. Long used to earning A's for minimal work, Craig had never developed a real sense of effort. Now, he was earning grades of 80 or less, but didn't know how to turn things around. After a few halfhearted attempts at trying harder, Craig concluded that expending extra energy had no real effect on his schoolwork. Instead, the boy began to wander around the room and disturb his classmates—behaviors that immediately earned him as much recognition as he formerly received for good grades. In no time, Craig was breaking nearly every classroom rule.

Craig's teacher understood that the boy's sudden turnaround had an emotional component. She quickly took steps to provide in-school support in reading and math, and suggested that Craig's parents work on their son's self-esteem and organizational skills. The teacher talked about the effects of Craig's misbehavior on the class, and explained that she was putting a time-out plan into effect which would help the boy stay focused on schoolwork. Any time Craig left his seat or interrupted his tablemates, he would be sent to a special desk at the side of the classroom. If he complied and worked quietly, he could return to the group when a timer sounded, nine minutes later. After less than a week of time-outs, Craig's wandering had completely stopped.

Chapter Six describes how to use the time-out approach in the classroom. Discussion is included about the ineffectiveness of threats, as well as things teachers can do to head off behavior problems that might require a discipline plan. You'll learn the fine points of putting the time-out technique in action, and find out how to involve parents to a greater degree. With some temporary extra effort, Craig's teacher was able to restore her students' ability to work quietly and without interruption. By putting the time-out approach to work in your classroom, you'll be able to minimize problem behavior, too.

Does the time-out approach have a place in the classroom? YES, say educators who believe in spending as little time as possible on student discipline. Isolating a student for a predetermined infraction discourages misbehavior in several ways. First, it attaches an immediate negative consequence to classroom antics. Second, it deprives the misbehaving student of her audience, thereby taking the fun out of causing a disturbance. Third, it pleases classmates and teachers alike by minimizing time taken from learning to correct behavior.

WHY THREATS DON'T WORK

Every time you warn a student against misbehaving, you undermine the effectiveness of the eventual consequence. Saying, "If you don't stop calling out/shredding paper/writing on the desk, I'll. . . ." teaches students that they don't have to comply with classroom rules right away. In fact, your words assure the rule-breaker that she can repeat the offending behavior several times before you'll actually step in. At that point, whatever consequence you assign lacks the impact it would have had as the price of the child's first infraction.

In addition, the use of threats can encourage your students to plead or bargain for additional chances. A child who has seen you fail to follow through in the face of student misbehavior is going to feel entitled to the same leniency whenever she breaks a rule. When a student's behavior causes problems in your classroom, issuing warnings instead of meting out consequences undermines the decisive air that's so important to your authority.

CIRCUMVENTING PROBLEMS

Of course, it's possible to head off a great deal of student misbehavior. Many times, inappropriate words and deeds are symptoms of temporary havoc in a child's life. Anger, exhaustion, or anxiety, for instance, can make a student feel rebellious, and lead to conduct that's out of the ordinary. Other times, a child in your class may simply begin testing your authority. Whatever the cause, a sudden lack of student cooperation can quickly become a habit. Here are some ideas for nipping problems in the bud.

HOW TO GIVE MORE EFFECTIVE INSTRUCTIONS

As every teacher knows, getting students to listen and act on what they're told is half the daily battle in any classroom. These tips can help you be more direct.

- ■ *Reclaim your students' attention.* Call daydreamers by name, and be animated and dynamic.

- ■ *Make extra eye contact.* Your steady gaze will hold that of your students.

- ■ *Speak with greater inflection.* A monotone is easily tuned out.

- ■ *Use shorter sentences.* Simple statements are the most arresting.

- ■ *Be more specific.* Think before you speak, and make every word count.

Children are a demanding audience. You're likely to find them most attentive when your instructions are long on enthusiasm and short on details.

- *Respond decisively.* Whether you answer or ask for time to think something over, do so with confidence. Hesitancy makes a teacher seem vulnerable, and encourages students to misbehave.

- *Respond without emotion.* Most student misbehavior is directed not at you personally, but at policies and rules. To a rebellious youngster, you serve not as a target, but as a figurehead of a system she dislikes.

- *Allow choices.* Giving students a sense of control does a lot to lessen boredom and frustration. As much as possible, run your class as a democracy.

- *Don't discipline the group.* It's usually counterproductive to penalize the entire class for a few students' misdeeds. Doing so angers the innocent and shelters the offenders.

- *Show confidence.* Convey rule-breaking as a challenge rather than a tiresome situation. Let your students know that you believe in their ability to make changes.

- *Spell things out.* Be clear about your rules and expectations. Helping students see the results of misbehavior on the group will clarify the need for self-control.

THWARTING AN ATTENTION-GETTER

Sometimes, students engage in minor misconduct simply to claim your attention, compelling you to waste time scolding and lecturing. However, there's an alternative. By withholding your reaction to minor infractions, you succeed in making the misbehavior pointless. Next time, try the following:

- Ignore annoying actions completely. Don't glance, glare, or say a word.

- Stand firm in your resolve to ignore. If you give in and respond, the student has won.

- State your position to the class. Ask them to join you in ignoring the annoying behavior.

- Be aware that the misconduct may escalate. Without attention, however, the student will soon feel somewhat foolish.

■ Return your attention when the student stops misbehaving. Let her know you're glad that she's rejoined the class.

Reacting to misbehavior encourages more of the same. By failing to recognize a student's minor pitches for attention, you'll take the fun out of annoying behavior.

■ *Be organized.* Do advance planning and setup to eliminate troublesome transitions and breaks in the action. Guard the flow of classroom activities carefully to avoid periods of idleness that can lead to misbehavior.

WHEN AND HOW TO USE TIME-OUT

Time-out in the classroom follows the same principle as time-out at home—that misbehavior is minimized when it leads to a swift, sure consequence. The technique is easy to put to work at school. And, just as when used at home, it becomes automatic when applied consistently. Described below are the steps needed to make time-out an effective mode of discipline.

1. *Establish a time-out area.* Designate a desk or study carrel as your classroom's isolation zone, keeping in mind the need to monitor the misbehaving student while at the same time depriving her of an audience. A seat at the side of the classroom often works well.

2. *Prepare take-home cards.* It's crucial to keep parents posted regarding a child's problem behavior, but doing so by phone or note can be discouragingly time-consuming. Instead, prepare a form on which you need only fill in blanks with the child's name, date, number of time-outs, and infraction(s).

3. *Explain your new approach.* The time-out consequence is most effective when it's discussed beforehand with parents and students. Discuss your feelings about the target misbehavior and its effect on the class, specify the purpose of the technique, and clarify the procedure you'll follow. In particular, tell parents how you'll be sending take-home cards.

4. *Give daily reminders.* At the beginning of each class, briefly discuss the misbehavior(s) that will result in time-out. Restate your goal of creating a disturbance-free environment by removing offenders from the group.

5. *Follow through.* When the target misconduct occurs, immediately isolate the guilty party for six to ten minutes—one minute per year of the student's age. Set a portable timer to signal the end of the time-out period, after which the child may return to her regular seat.

6. *Stay in control.* If the child dawdles or refuses to go to the isolation area, calmly add one minute to her time-out. Wait twenty seconds and, if necessary, tell her that she has earned an additional minute. Be matter-of-fact, and turn your attention back to the class after each statement.

7. *Put responsibility where it belongs.* If the misbehaving child still won't comply with your directive to go to time-out, quietly inform her that recess and other applicable privileges are suspended until her time-out is served. Then, withdraw your attention.

8. *Fill out a take-home card*. Start a parents' update form the first time a child goes to time-out. At day's end, complete and sign it, and send it home for the child's parents to review and sign.

When a teacher employs the time-out technique, parental review of take-home forms is an important component with built-in stumbling blocks. First, you may occasionally encounter a family that is uninterested in the issue of school behavior. If you find you're not getting parental support, it's appropriate to discontinue sending take-home notes to that family. Instead, redouble your emphasis on the child's importance to classroom dynamics and your delight in her acceptable behavior. In cases where a child routinely loses, hides, or ignores her take-home form, you may wish to consider taking an additional step. Tell the child's parents to expect a form every day, regardless of school conduct. If there are no incidents of misbehavior, say so with a star or sticker.

Isolating a child for a predetermined infraction takes the fun out of misbehaving. Using time-out as a consequence works well in the classroom because it downplays incidences

RIGHTS AND RESPONSIBILITIES

Today's students know a lot about their rights in the classroom, but they sometimes forget that these entitlements belong to fellow students and the teacher, as well. You may find it helpful to remind your class of the following issues.

■ You have the right to disagree, but you may not do so disrespectfully.

■ You have the right to be recognized, but you must find positive ways to gain attention.

■ You have the right to succeed, but you must do so graciously.

■ You have the right to social contact, but you must keep conversation within the context of classwork.

■ You have the right to your individuality, but you may not ignore your responsibility to classmates.

Students may find ordinary ground rules more meaningful when they're presented as part of a framework of social behavior.

THOMAS'S CHOICE

"Last fall, I had occasion to coach Thomas, a very capable second grader, through a tough written assignment. After that, he wanted me beside him all the time and refused to work alone. I tried reasoning with him, rewarding him, cheering him on . . . just about any tactic you could think of. Finally, I decided that his refusal to work alone would have to have consequences.

After telling Thomas to call me only with specific questions, I reminded him that the class had a set amount of time to complete each assignment. I explained that from now on, if Thomas finished his work on time, he could do an errand for me (a coveted privilege in second grade). If he did not, he would have to serve a seven-minute time-out and complete the assignment when he returned to his seat.

The change in Thomas's attitude was immediate. Once I distanced myself and handed the responsibility for doing seatwork to Thomas, he found the wherewithal to settle down and concentrate. I've used this approach for three months now, and in that time, Thomas has only gone overtime once."

Glenda Parker,
Second-grade teacher

of misconduct without compromising school standards. It also turns the teacher's focus from the offending student back to the lesson or activity at hand. Not only does time-out protect the group from the aftermath of one student's misbehavior, it places responsibility for self-control squarely on the shoulders of the offender.

7
Variations

Lindy, age seven, and her brother Greg, age nine, are frequently at odds. While each is undeniably the other's best friend, the amount of time the two spend playing together makes daily conflict a certainty. Whether the siblings are engrossed in a project, howling over a silly game, or just relaxing in front of the TV, there's an ongoing struggle for control. As the pair's father puts it, "They're either getting along famously, or killing each other." Recently, Lindy and Greg's arguments took a hurtful turn, including shoving, name-calling, and derision. The parents tried sorting out these worsening conflicts,

*but found each child protesting his or her innocence
and blaming the other.*

*The psychologist at the children's grade school
proposed the idea of a double time-out. When Lindy
and Greg's arguments turned nasty, the parents
were to separate and isolate both children—without
discussion. Timing out both offenders, the psychologist reasoned, would make it clear that hostility is
unacceptable, and divide responsibility for the confrontation equally between the children. At first,
Lindy and Greg protested vehemently when both
were held responsible for battles that turned hostile.
However, after just a handful of double time-outs,
the pair concluded that it's no longer possible to
goad one another into punishable behavior and
escape unscathed. They've begun hammering out
more reasonable approaches to their conflicts.*

*Chapter Seven provides information on double
time-outs and other variations on the time-out technique. You'll learn when and why these variations
are useful, and get information on how to put each
approach to use. In addition, you'll get the lowdown
on the point at which everyday squabbles become
inappropriate, and bothersome behaviors that don't
merit a time-out. Lindy and Greg have resumed
their old comradeship, much to their parents'
delight. By employing the alternative tactics discussed in this chapter, you, too, can address special
situations that may crop up at home.*

Much has been said in earlier chapters about the need to be consistent in your use of time-out. Indeed, studies have shown that putting the tactic to work in the same manner, and for the same reason, every time is often the surest way to help your child police his behavior. There are situations, however, when a variation of the time-out technique actually increases its effectiveness. The how's and why's of three alternative tactics are described below.

DOUBLE TIME-OUT

When two children get in trouble together, or when an everyday squabble between them suddenly intensifies, it's common practice for the adult in charge to step in. By assuming the role of judge and jury, however, you take on the responsibility for solving the problem. Of course, it's difficult to address an infraction that you didn't see, or to judge a conflict that involves a dramatic or highly verbal child. Nevertheless, children who count on parental intervention may be more likely to provoke one another or start a conflict just to get your attention. In addition, they'll likely scramble to prove their innocence and the other's guilt.

To make the situation easier to manage, you may wish to try sending both children to time-out at once. Doing so downplays the cause of the conflict, which may be impossible to accurately assess anyway, and enables you to withhold, rather than give, attention to inappropriate conduct. When both parties endure the same consequence, they're inspired to find more acceptable solutions to their disagreements. You can employ double time-out as follows.

1. Praise the children's cooperative behavior at every opportunity. Help them to feel proud of their ability to work and play as a team.

2. Be sure that both children understand the concept of time-out. They'll be less inclined to protest if they've been isolated for misbehavior before.

3. Declare time-out at a moment when both children are actively involved in the situation. This way, no one can feel like a victim.

4. Send each offender to a spot out of the other's sight. Place the timer between them.

5. Set the timer according to the younger child's age—say, six minutes for youngsters who are six and eight years old.

WHEN DOES CONFLICT BECOME UNACCEPTABLE?

When two children are at odds, the point at which you step in is largely a matter of tolerance. Here are some general guidelines on when to consider calling a time-out.

- When a confrontation turns physical.
- When name-calling or other cruelty is involved.
- When one child is clearly provoking the other.
- When the argument is familiar and too frequent.
- When a younger or less-verbal child is overmatched.

On a cautionary note, it's important to stick with your personal criteria for time-out. If you isolate children sooner than usual when you're distracted or feeling irritable, you won't fool anyone. Your children will perceive that time-out is a device for you, not them.

6. Give the pair responsibility for leaving
   time-out when the bell rings.

Employing double time-out spares you the
task of determining which child is in the
wrong. The technique also sends a clear mes-
sage that both parties share responsibility for
their unacceptable behavior.

TIME-OUT FOR OBJECTS

There's no denying the fact that toys occasionally get misused by children. When conditions
are right, they're flung, kicked, used as
weapons, and fought over. Household gadgets
and appliances are fodder for parent/child
strife, as well. When sharing or inappropriate
usage becomes an issue, there's an excellent
alternative to timing out your child. Instead,
isolate the object for the usual length of time.
This technique is gentler than repeatedly disciplining a child for unacceptable but age-
appropriate behavior. And, it's especially
effective when several children are involved in
the misdeed.

   Timing out a toy or object teaches warring
playmates that both parties lose by fighting. It
also makes clear the fact that anything used in

a reckless or forbidden manner will be confiscated. The potential for losing a plaything—even for a few minutes—will compel your child to practice self-control, and will motivate a pair or group of children to resolve disputes in acceptable ways. Best of all, this alternative spares you the worry that your child's behavior is earning him too much time in isolation. The next time your child fights over or abuses a toy or gadget, here's what you can do.

1. As you approach your child, don't be drawn into the conflict. You're stepping in not to debate, but to initiate an earned consequence.

2. Place the confiscated item in view but out of your child's reach. Put the portable timer where your child can see it, and set it to your child's age.

3. If the abused object is too large to move—if your child was kicking the TV, for example—place the timer next to it to declare it temporarily off limits.

4. Explain why you've placed the toy or object in time-out. Use as few words as possible, and don't indulge in conversation.

WHEN *NOT* TO DECLARE TIME-OUT

The time-out technique is amazingly effective against aggressive, rude, or otherwise unacceptable behavior, but it shouldn't always be the tactic of choice. The following misbehaviors, some mood-driven, others personality-based, are more unpleasant than inappropriate and, as such, are not opportunities for time-out.

- Grouchiness
- Restlessness
- Poor motivation
- Overactivity
- Reclusiveness
- Sullenness
- Irresponsibility
- Timidity
- Clinginess

In addition, it's not advisable to call time-out for infractions that you didn't fully witness. If a misdeed happens nearby, it's possible that the report you hear or your own perception may be inaccurate. A resultant time-out may be grossly unfair.

5. Return the item when the timer rings, with the reminder that an alternative behavior is needed.

6. If your child repeats the misdeed, follow through with another time-out. Losing access to the object a second time should convince him that you mean business.

Time-out for objects is an excellent way to curb abusive or overly aggressive play. Isolating a plaything is every bit as effective as banishing a child, and is a good way to focus on a new or particularly dangerous habit that needs changing.

PARENTAL TIME-OUT

Every parent knows how easily worry or a bad day can undermine one's ability to cope with the demands of caring for children. When your nerves are frayed, even total compliance on your child's part may not be enough to restore your sense of self-control. At this point, in fact, you may be at risk of venting your frustration with words or actions that you'll regret later. A respite—a parental time-out—is the perfect solution.

It's no secret that escalating anger can lead to berating or striking a child. But, did you know that many youngsters find even moderate adult anger frightening? Your worsening mood can trigger a rush of insecurity in your child, who correctly senses your fragile state and feels insecure as a result. When you feel stressed, little problems are magnified and quickly add to your annoyance. Taking a time-out—that is, putting space between you and your child and collecting your thoughts—can help you put an aggravating situation in perspective. In addition, you set a wonderful example for your child when you emerge from time-out refreshed and recharged. Here's what to do.

1. Decide in advance how far away from your child you can safely go. His age and your home's layout are the chief determinants of your time-out's location.

2. Review your options. A quick shower? A phone call to an understanding friend? A coffee break? Decide which activity you'd find most rejuvenating.

3. Tell your child when you feel overwrought. Explain that you need some time by yourself to calm down.

THE GETAWAY

"We use time-outs, and I've found that they are effective for me, too. When my first child was very small, he was very demanding. I can recall quite a few times when I'd just put him in his crib and go outside into the woods to scream—never far from the house, but away from my son.

Five minutes is not very long. You can make sure your child is safe out of your sight, and though he may cry when you leave him, he'll be just fine when you return. He'll appreciate your calm demeanor, too."

Stephen Harris
Editor/Publisher,
Full-Time Dads

4. Set a portable timer for ten minutes and place it where your child can see it.

5. When the timer rings, find your child immediately and reassure him that all is well.

By distancing yourself from your child when you feel frazzled, you teach an important lesson in self-control. In addition, you get the chance to regain your emotional grip so that you can proceed with the day's events without harming or scaring your child.

Time-out is an effective discipline approach that can be tailored to different circumstances without minimizing its effectiveness against child misbehavior. You'll have proof of this after trying the variations described above. If you keep the ground rules of consistency, immediacy, and even-temperedness in mind, you can successfully develop other adaptations to fit your family's needs.

8
The Flip Side

From the time she was born, Alyssa, a high-strung child now six years old, threw things whenever she got angry. Frustrating toys were flung across the room, along with spurned foods, challenging school-work, and garments with intricate fastenings. When first grade saw Alyssa still hurling anything that thwarted her, the girl's parents instituted the time-out technique. Any time Alyssa vented anger by throwing something, she was banished for six minutes to the laundry alcove off her family's kitchen. The forced inactivity was so unpleasant that she broke her throwing habit almost at once.

Pleased as Alyssa's father was to see the object-throwing come to an end, he was certain that his excitable daughter needed another way to handle her flashes of anger. He decided to teach Alyssa to vent her fury by pounding her pillow when at home, and by striking her heels together when at school or out in public. At their family doctor's urging, he made it a point to notice and offer praise whenever the little girl exhibited self-control or chose an acceptable outlet for her anger. So effective was the father's effort to reinforce desirable behavior that he began pointing out the many other things his daughter did right. Bolstered by her dad's words of approval, Alyssa's self-esteem and tolerance for frustration took an immediate upswing.

In Chapter Eight, you'll learn how and why to reinforce your child's episodes of desirable conduct in addition to using time-outs. The strategies presented will encourage communication, give your child the tools to deal with adversity, and help you remain in control of behavioral situations. Information is also provided to help you boost your child's self-image and reward her efforts at good conduct. With positive reinforcement, Alyssa learned to manage her anger and see herself in a new, acceptable light. The material in Chapter Eight can help you similarly refocus your child's energy.

In the adult world, awards, raises, and performance reviews are an employer's way of reinforcing good work and solid effort—your equivalent of the behavior most parents want to see exhibited by their children. Just as positive feedback keeps you on track, so it does with your youngster's conduct.

Children, of course, love attention in any form. Why else would they act out when angry, bored, or frustrated? It follows, then, that a positive gesture from you following an episode of good behavior on your child's part will encourage her to continue to behave in the same fashion. And as a bonus, commending your child for what she does right enables you to counteract the matter-of-factness of time-out with plenty of smiles and warmth.

HOW TO INCREASE YOUR CHILD'S GOOD CONDUCT

To help encourage more acceptable behavior, you need to convince your youngster of only one thing: Socially appropriate words and actions merit the attention and approval of both adults and children. The key to persuading your child that this is so lies in giving

TEN THINGS TO SAY TO YOUR CHILD EVERY DAY

"Accentuate the positive," urges an old song—and the idea of using positive statements to elicit positive behavior is a perfect example. Listed below are ten phrases that work wonders in reinforcing your child's good conduct and self-control.

1. *"That's a good way to solve your problem."* It's important to give credit where it's due. Children need to know when they've made wise choices.

2. *"I like the tone of voice you're using."* Is your child a screamer? Does she tend toward rudeness or sarcasm? She'll learn from your praise of her efforts to use a normal tone.

3. *"You're feeling angry/anxious, aren't you?"* When you acknowledge your child's negative moods, you make a bad situation more tolerable.

4. *"Remember, there's no hitting/grabbing allowed."* You can help your child control aggression by reminding her of the behavior you expect.

5. *"I know it's hard to share/wait on line."* Commiserating with your child's impatient side shows that you understand her annoyance and makes it easier to handle.

6. *"It's a big help when you dress yourself/clean up your toys."* Children love knowing that their assistance is important and appreciated.

7. *"I'm so proud that you're pedaling your tricycle/doing multiplication by yourself."* It's hard work reaching childhood milestones, so give your youngster time in the spotlight when she does.

8. *"It's nice to be around you because you're so cheerful/energetic."* It's good for your child to recognize the characteristics that draw others to her.

9. *"You're so good at skateboarding/drawing."* Your child's talents help her stand out in a crowd. It's good to make her aware of these strengths.

10. *"One of the things that makes you special is your sense of humor/kindness."* Let your youngster know when her interactions and behavior have positive results.

It's good for children to be reminded of their good qualities. When you remark on the positive things your child does, you're likely to see more of this admirable behavior.

immediate positive feedback each time she does something good. Here are three important steps.

1. *Be aware of your child's appropriate behavior.* Did your youngster respond immediately to a request? Play quietly while you were busy with a sibling? Get through a

play date without fighting with her guest? Even though these are expected behaviors, they deserve your praise. Positive attention will reduce your child's need for the spotlight.

2. *Step up your physical contact.* When possible, stay close enough to your child to offer physical reassurance, affection, and attention. Gestures such as hair-tousling, loving pats, hugs, high fives, and shoulder massages help your child feel loved and secure and lessen her need to gain attention by acting up.

3. *Use social rewards.* Attach positive consequences to your child's appropriate behavior. Praise is very effective, of course, as is the charting of points toward a special treat. You can also extend privileges, or keep on hand a collection of discount-store "prizes" to award. Other good-conduct rewards include time spent with you or the chance to pursue a favorite activity.

When your child experiences firsthand the dividends that follow incidents of desirable behavior, she'll surely be convinced of the importance of self-control.

REWARDS THAT WORK

Children find tangible feedback very inspiring. However, compensating your child for admirable behavior doesn't have to cost a lot. Here are some rewards your youngster will enjoy.

An on-the-spot story

A favorite dessert

A family bike ride

Water play at the sink

A game of her choosing

A video rental

Having a friend sleep over

Ten extra minutes past bedtime

A trip to the park

A pack of clay or chalk

Points toward a prize

Cookie- or brownie-baking

TACTICS FOR ENCOURAGING GOOD BEHAVIOR

Rewards given for what your child does right are even more effective when paired with strategies meant to keep the good behavior coming. The child who earns praise five times a day, for instance, will understand what's expected of her sooner than the child whose behavior warrants positive feedback only once or twice per week. What follows is a collection of tactics for stepping up your child's noteworthy conduct.

Think of Alternatives to Inappropriate Behavior

Help your child think of suitably appropriate behaviors. If she tends to hit or bite, suggest that she vent her aggression on a pillow. If she often screams in anger, teach her to take a deep breath and use words to convey her feelings. If rude talk is a problem, suggest that your child put her anger on paper, either in words or a picture. With a physical outlet for her frustration, she'll be less likely to explode.

Make Changes in Your Child's Environment

You can make good behavior easier for your child by making small changes in her environment. Cut down on "No's"—and the potential for conflict—by moving fragile or dangerous items out of your child's way. Arrange your youngster's toys, clothing, and grooming tools in a manner that invites self-sufficiency. Be it snack time or homework time, let your child be as independent as possible.

Always Spell Out the Expected Behavior

Even if you're embarking on a familiar activity, never leave your child's conduct to chance. At the last minute, explain what's about to take place, and describe in detail what you expect of your child. Mention the consequences of misbehavior, but remind your youngster that you have faith in her.

Ignore Random Misbehavior

Make interaction between you and your child as positive as possible by overlooking minor misconduct that is out of the ordinary. Without reacting at all, turn your back and direct your attention elsewhere. Give your child some positive attention the moment the misbehavior stops.

Teach Your Child to Comfort Herself

Teach your child to look on the bright side—"I didn't win the contest, but I was among the top four entrants"—and offer sympathy when she feels thwarted by circumstance. Eventually, she'll learn the art of soothing herself, and will experience far less frustration as a result.

Set a Good Example

Remember that your behavior serves as a model for your child. Take pains to treat people with respect and to act on opportunities to be helpful and giving. Acknowledge your anger, but express it appropriately, and avoid the use of sarcasm, insults, and foul language.

Never React to Your Child in Anger

When you direct your annoyance at your child, it's easy to lose control and use words that are insulting or cruel. A young or sensitive child, in particular, may interpret your harsh tone or wild-eyed look as a sign that you no longer care about her.

Help Your Youngster Rise Above Her Failures

Help your child practice the skills she finds difficult. For example, if your child struggles with multiplication, practice a different "times" table every day, aloud and on a calculator. As the facts begin to sound familiar, your child will gain confidence and realize that she will soon catch up with her classmates.

Look for Hidden Explanations

The reasons for your child's misbehavior may not always be obvious. If misbehavior is on the rise, help your child recognize the emotions that lie behind her change of conduct. During a calm moment, ask whether your youngster is worried about something, or whether something has gone wrong in school or with a friend.

SKIRTING THE PITFALLS

Every parent knows of a few situations that act as triggers for inappropriate or annoying conduct on their child's part. Some common problem areas are listed below, along with suggestions for minimizing their potential for troublesome behavior.

- ■ *Telephone calls.* Whether animated or businesslike, a phone conversation takes your attention away from your child. If you store a basket of odds and ends—junk mail, stampers and a pad, beads and string, and so on—near your telephone, you'll be able to divert your child, as well.

- ■ *Waiting on lines.* Many errands involve waiting, which is hardly a child's strong suit. Diversion is the best way to help your impatient youngster pass the time, so pack a tote bag with books, a yo-yo, small cars, and other activities that require little space.

■ *Car trips.* The younger the child, the more bored she is by riding in a car. Before your next trip, help your youngster fill a backpack with snacks, and lap-sized toys and games. If you stockpile catalogs from toy companies, you can add the latest issue as a surprise.

■ *Health-care visits.* In advance, share books about the doctor or dentist. Schedule checkups for your child's cheeriest time of day, and phone ahead to see if the doctor is running on schedule. Bring toys for the waiting room and a doll for practice "exams."

■ *Haircuts.* The scissors, the shaver, the vinyl drape—there's a lot to dislike about a haircut. Make an advance visit to prepare your child, and have her bring a security object to hold on the big day. Stand beside your child, or even hold her in your lap, during her cut.

"WHAT ABOUT ME?"

"I never realized how I took my daughter's good behavior for granted till she began acting up when her little brother was about six months old. Almost overnight, my obedient first-born became rude, impatient, and defiant. However, we dismissed the idea of jealousy, since the baby had been around for a while. It took an observant friend to point out that my son might be more of a threat to his sister as a determined (and very cute) crawler than when he'd just sat around. She may have been misbehaving simply to get her fair share of attention.

We resolved to start noticing my daughter more. When she began collecting praise for being pleasant, helpful, and well-behaved, she returned immediately to her sweet, good-natured self.

Daria H., mother of two
Via the Internet

Spend at Least Ten Minutes a Day Enjoying Your Child

Set aside some time to do positive things with your child. Balance the time you spend teaching, quizzing, demonstrating, and modifying her behavior with time spent at play. Relax, let your child choose what to do, and let yourself remember the many reasons why your youngster delights you.

The more attention you give to your child's appropriate words and deeds, the more you'll convince her of the merits of continuing to behave in this manner. Help her feel good about being good, and she'll strive even harder for self-control. Moreover, she'll soon have a repertoire of positive conduct to use in place of the behaviors you target for time-outs.

Conclusion

C hildren lack the emotional stamina to sort
through their feelings, which are often as
powerful as they are fleeting. Hysterical laugh-
ter one minute—a storm of tears the next—
with so many ups and downs, it's no wonder
that some youngsters rely on hostility or nasty
words to let off steam.

Of course, aggressive behavior is often con-
sidered inappropriate. Learning to hold childish emotions in check, and to search for acceptable outlets for the most overwhelming of
them, are giant steps toward the self-control

expected by society. If your child is among the many who struggle to understand this very important lesson, the time-out approach is the perfect solution. Does your child misbehave with regularity? You can extinguish her misconduct by attaching a sure, swift, humane consequence—a time-out—to each offense. There's no better choice for parents eager to shape their child's behavior without anger and humiliation.

As you've learned from this book, the time-out technique is as simple as it is effective. Identify your child's problem behavior, select a time-out location, and explain that isolation in the agreed-upon area will now follow each infraction. For every incidence thereafter, declare a time-out in a businesslike tone and set a portable timer. Let your child be in control of serving her time and resuming play when the timer goes off.

Will the misbehavior in question vanish overnight? Probably not, childish impulsiveness being what it is. However, if you're consistent in responding to the target misdeed with a neutral consequence—isolation—rather than with emotion or debate, your child will discover that breaking rules is no longer rewarding. Rather than act out to grab a piece of the limelight—in this case, Mom's or Dad's attention—your child will be convinced to toe the line and earn postive feedback, instead.

Once you remove emotion from the art of disciplining your child, thwarting the adult in charge loses much of its appeal. If you add a healthy dose of praise for admirable behavior, you'll eliminate power struggles and shift the balance of your parent/child interactions in a positive direction. Used correctly, the time-out approach has had a dramatic effect on many family relationships. Put the technique to work in your home, and see what it does for you!

Suggested Readings

A parent can never have too many resources. The publications listed below are an excellent source of support and information to help you in your endeavor to guide your child's behavior.

BOOKS

Clark, Lynn, Ph.D. *SOS! Help for Parents*. Bowling Green, KY: Parents Press, 1985.

Clark, Lynn, Ph.D. *The Time-Out Solution*. Chicago: Contemporary Books, 1989.

Crary, Elizabeth. *Love and Limits: Guidance Tools for Creative Parenting*. Seattle, WA: Parenting Press, 1994.

Crary, Elizabeth. *365 Wacky, Wonderful Ways to Get Your Child to Do What You Want*. Seattle, WA: Parenting Press, 1994.

Crary, Elizabeth. *Without Spanking or Spoiling: A Practical Approach to Toddler and Preschool Guidance.* Seattle, WA: Parenting Press, 1993.

Hill, Barbara Albers. *Baby Tactics: Parenting Tips That Really Work.* Garden City Park, NY: Avery Publishing Group, 1991.

Kersey, Katharine C. *Don't Take It Out On Your Kids: A Parent's Guide to Positive Discipline.* New York: Berkley Books, 1994.

Lighter, Dawn. *Gentle Discipline: 50 Effective Techniques for Teaching Your Child Good Behavior.* Deephaven, MN: Meadowbrook Press, 1995.

Schwarzchild, Michael. *Helping Your Difficult Child Behave: A Guide to Improving Children's Self-Control Without Losing Your Own.* Rocklin, CA: Prima, 1995.

Sears, William, M.D. *The Discipline Book: Everything You Need to Know to Have a Better Behaved Child From Birth to Age 10.* New York: Little, Brown, & Co., 1995.

Varni, James W., Ph.D and Donna G. Corwin. *Time-Out for Toddlers.* New York: Berkley Books, 1991.

PUBLICATIONS

Bierman, Jack. Editor-in-Chief. *L.A. Parent* (magazine). P.O. Box 3204, Burbank, CA 91504.

Cook, Sally, Publisher and Editor. *Central California Parent (magazine).* 2037 W. Bullard, #131, Fresno, CA 93711-1200.

Harris, Stephen, Editor/Publisher. *Full-Time Dads (newsletter).* P.O. Box 577, Cumberland, ME 04021.

Index

117